Financial Advisor Safeguard Volume 1

How to Protect Yourself, Your Practice and Your Aging Clients Who Have Diminished Mental Capacity

Bob Mauterstock, CFP®

BizSmart Publishing
ORANGE, TEXAS, USA

Copyright Published by BizSmart Publishing
2725 23RD St, Orange, TX 77630
support@bizsmartmedia.com

Copyright © 2016 Robert Mauterstock
Cover Design © 2016 Nathan Dasco, http://nathanieldasco.com/

All Rights Reserved No part of this publication or the information in it may be quoted from or reproduced in any form by means such as printing, scanning, photocopying or otherwise without prior written permission of the authors except as provided by the United States of America copyright law.

CFP® Safeguard: How to Protect Yourself, Your Practice and Your Aging Clients Who Have Diminished Mental Capacity/Bob Mauterstock. -- 1st ed.
ISBN-13: 978-1537705101
ISBN-10: 1537705105

Disclaimer and Terms of Use: Effort has been made to ensure that the information in this book is accurate and complete; however, the author and the publisher do not warrant the accuracy of the information, text and graphics contained within the book due to the rapidly changing nature of science, research, known and unknown facts and internet. The Author and the publisher do not hold any responsibility for errors, omissions or contrary interpretation of the subject matter herein. This book is presented solely for motivational and informational purposes only. The Publisher has strived to be as accurate and complete as possible in the creation of this book.

This book is not intended for use as a source of legal, business, accounting or financial advice. All readers are advised to seek services of competent professionals in legal, business, accounting, and finance field. In practical advice books, like anything else in life, there are no guarantees of income made. Readers are cautioned to rely on their own judgment about their individual circumstances to act accordingly.

While all attempts have been made to verify information provided in this publication, the Publisher assumes no responsibility for errors, omissions, or contrary interpretation of the subject matter herein. Any perceived slights of specific persons, peoples, or organizations are unintentional. For more information, please visit http://www.BizSmartPublishing.com

DEDICATION

I would like to dedicate this book to my mom, Ruth Mauterstock, who lived with the Alzheimer's disease for ten years. Up to the end she was a sweet, compassionate and loving person who addressed everyone in her life as "Dearie."

ACKNOWLEDGEMENTS

I'd like to acknowledge the aides and staff of Harbor Point at Centerville for their tireless dedication to the residents of their community. They are truly angels. Harbor Point at Centerville is the first residential assisted living community on Cape Cod exclusively dedicated to serving the needs of individuals with memory loss.

I'd also like to acknowledge the staff of Broad Reach Hospice for the loving support they gave my mom. Their hospice program helped her to live out her last days with dignity and love.

TABLE OF CONTENTS

Chapter 1: Entering The Perfect Storm 1

Chapter 2: Step One: Recognizing Unusual Behavior Patterns You See In Your Clients 3

Chapter 3: Step Two: Initiating A Specific Series Of Steps To Protect You And Your Client 7

Chapter 4: Step Three: Creating Long-Term Care Plans For Your Clients 9

Chapter 5: Step Four: Building A Network Of Professionals 23

Chapter 6: Step Five: Building A Relationship With The Family 25

Chapter 7: Step Six: Utilize A Single Source Record-Keeping Document 29

Chapter 8: Step Seven: Creating An Investment Policy Statement ... 31

Chapter 9: Concluding Thoughts 33

FORWARD

When Bob came to present to FPA Massachusetts in 2013, his message resonated with our members.

The importance of his message of communicating, "passing the torch," and leaving a legacy resonated with every advisor both personally and professionally.

Hearing Bob and his own personal story of his mother's struggle with Alzheimer's disease hit home. Everyone in the room could relate his story to a family member or loved one.

Bob's passion for eldercare and protecting our families from financial abuse is unprecedented, and he knows communication is a vital gift we can give to our families and our clients.

Since then, Bob has gone on to present to hundreds of financial advisors and share this important roadmap to advisors and their clients. He has been an avid educator and proponent of families communicating and planning their future together.

Through the gift of communication, we can affect how our families are cared for, for generations to come. The time is now to have those conversations with families and trusted advisors. It is a gift that will remain far after we have passed on.

Kristin Bean, Executive Director
Financial Planning Association of Massachusetts

FREE GIFT FOR READERS

As a bonus for my readers, I'd like to offer you a free gift. My free PDF guide, *The LifeFolio System®: Six Steps to Organizing Your Life with the LifeFolio System®*, will help you get all of your important papers and information in order before disaster strikes. It is available for download at http://www.LifeFolioSystem.com.

During my 33-year career as a financial advisor, I observed many clients who were facing a family emergency and couldn't find the important documents and information they needed to get things done to handle their affairs.

Whether you are changing jobs, buying a home, caring for an aging loved one, experiencing a death in the family, or planning your retirement, events can send you into a document search tailspin. Just think about how many documents the bank requests when you apply for your home mortgage or the litany of current and historical documents that are needed to settle an estate when someone has died.

Because we don't tend to deliberately sit down and document everything we have or might need to prepare for such events, unexpected circumstances send most of us scurrying to collect what is required.

Get your copy today at http://www.LifeFolioSystem.com.

ONE

ENTERING THE PERFECT STORM

You, as a financial advisor, are about to enter the perfect storm.

Several factors are lining up to make the next ten years the most challenging years that you will ever face in your practice. Consider these facts:

- Your clients are living longer than their parents.
- The fastest growing age group are the very old, those people over 85.
- The Alzheimer's Association has predicted that 46% of those people over age 85 will develop some form of dementia.
- It is expected that 10 million baby boomers will develop Alzheimer's. Unless we find a treatment or a cure, Alzheimer's will become the defining disease of the Baby Boom Generation.
- One in eight baby boomers will get the disease after they turn 65. At age 85 that risk increases to nearly one in two. And if they don't have it, chances are they will likely be caring for someone who does.

Have you already had to deal with a client with diminished capacity? What did you do?

Does your firm have a standard protocol or procedure to deal with those clients?

I have spoken to a number of financial planning groups around the country. Each time I speak I ask the audience, "How many of you have had to deal with a client who is demonstrating diminished mental capacity?" About half the people in the audience raise their hands. Then I ask them a second question, "How many of you have a standard procedure to deal with clients who have this condition?" Only one or two people respond.

Most of us are traveling blind into this abyss! **Practicing without a plan for mental incapacity is like holding a ticking time bomb.** Sooner or later it is going to go off and a client or client's family will go after you for handling their account improperly.

In 2009 Fidelity surveyed 350 advisors. More than 84% indicated that they had been touched by someone in their client base who suffers from Alzheimer's Disease. **Despite their experience with the disease, more than 96% of the advisors did not feel that they were prepared to assist clients with Alzheimer's.** And things have not changed since that survey. Very few firms have stepped forward with specific guidelines for their advisors to deal with diminished capacity.

And that is why I have written this book. Based on my experience of over thirty-three years as a financial advisor, I will give you the seven steps that you can take to minimize the risk to you and your practice and take the appropriate actions to serve your clients with diminished capacity.

So let's get started!

TWO

STEP ONE: RECOGNIZING UNUSUAL BEHAVIOR PATTERNS YOU SEE IN YOUR CLIENTS

No one is expecting you to be able to diagnose dementia. But if you have been working with a client for any period of time, you will learn their behavior patterns and notice if they have changed.

If a client who has always been early for appointments begins showing up late or missing appointments altogether, you should take note. Or if a client begins to have difficulty following directions or filling out forms, it will become evident. Other indicators include frequent calls to the office, repeatedly asking the same question, or having difficulty recalling past decisions or actions. Isolated examples of these behaviors may not create concern, but repeated patterns should trigger close scrutiny.

We began becoming concerned about my mother when my wife took her to a doctor's appointment. My mom had been a patient of the same doctor for over thirteen years. The doctor's long-term nurse greeted my mom with "How are you, Ruth?" and my mother responded with "Do I know you?" That began a series of patterns that made it clear my mother was slipping.

She began having difficulties finding the dining hall of the retirement residence she lived it. She was selectively taking medication each day based on what she thought she needed. She often became dehydrated because she wasn't drinking enough water. As a result of all these incidents, we decided to bring her back to her doctor who diagnosed her with Alzheimer's.

The first problem I had with a client involved a physician who I had been working with for over twenty years. He was an extremely competent anesthesiologist who had attended Harvard Medical School and was highly regarded in the community. A few years after he retired, he began calling my office asking to speak to his accountant. My assistant reminded him several times that his accountant was not in our office. But he kept calling.

This behavior was very unusual for him. I realized that there was a problem. Unfortunately, I did not feel I had the authority to break his confidentiality and call his spouse or children to ask if he was having memory problems. I was able to call his accountant and asked him if the doctor had spoken with him recently.

The accountant revealed that he had noticed the doctor's erratic behavior and confusion dealing with his tax return. He mentioned to me that my client had made an appointment to see his estate planning attorney in the next few weeks and I might want to give the attorney a call.

I called the attorney, who acknowledged that she was meeting with my client and his wife in the next few weeks. I expressed my concern and suggested that we set up a family meeting with the client, his wife and children to do some planning together. She agreed.

A few weeks later we had a meeting with the client and his family and it became readily apparent during the course of the meeting that he was confused and having memory issues. At the meeting we were able to outline a course of action to support him that involved the whole family.

I will discuss procedures for having a meaningful family meeting in Chapter 6.

THREE

STEP TWO: INITIATING A SPECIFIC SERIES OF STEPS TO PROTECT YOU AND YOUR CLIENT

If you have a suspicion that a client is demonstrating unusual behavior and may be losing mental capacity, you should take the following steps:

1. **Share your concerns with other members of your staff and your supervisor if you have one.** Note if they have observed similar unusual actions.
2. **Make notes of all future interactions with the client, phone calls, meetings.** Save emails and correspondence.
3. Review client's file:
   a. Does the client have a Durable Power of Attorney? Who is listed as the holder of that power? Is there a provision in the Durable Power for incapacity?
   b. Does the client have any trusts? Is he the trustee of his own trust? Is there a provision in the trust document for replacement of trustee if incapacity is demonstrated?

4. **Request that the client identify a client advocate.** This could be the holder of the durable power, a listed successor trustee or a friend or advisor. Explain that firm procedure is to request that all clients identify a client advocate. Have the client sign a form authorizing you to share client information with the advocate.

5. **Invite the client advocate to all future meetings with the client.** Do not meet with the client alone.

6. **Include another advisor or associate in all future meetings with the client.**

If the client refuses to include a client advocate in future meetings, will not create a Durable Power of Attorney and resists all your efforts to protect him, consider firing the client.

FOUR

STEP THREE: CREATING LONG-TERM CARE PLANS FOR YOUR CLIENTS

If one of your clients is stricken with Alzheimer's or some form of dementia, it is important for you to help your client develop a long-term care plan for their care. There are three basic questions that you must ask your client

Question 1. How will you pay for your care?

Medicare

When I ask clients how they will pay for long-term care, many have responded, "We have Medicare. Shouldn't that cover our health care costs?" However, most of them do not realize that they must spend at least three nights in a hospital and be referred by their physician to be covered by Medicare, and coverage is limited strictly to rehabilitation (skilled care),

Medicare will cover the expenses (with a co-pay) incurred by a person 65 or older for up to one hundred days in a rehab facility. The average Medicare-covered stay is twenty-two days. And Medicare will provide limited coverage for expenses incurred for rehabilitation if you choose to go home.

Medicare covers up to thirty-five hours a week of skilled nursing care and home health aide services at home. You may also receive additional hours of skilled physical and occupational therapy and other social services. The amount of care allowed in the plan of care depends on your doctor's recommendation.

Realistically, based on what Medicare pays the home health care agencies, you can expect to receive about ten hours of care per week at home. Services and supplies approved in the plan of care are covered in full. Durable medical equipment is covered at 80% of the Medicare-approved amount. **But please note: Medicare will not cover chronic or custodial care if you are not expected to recover.** Your doctor or the rehab facility generally makes that determination.

Medicaid

Many people are confused about the differences between Medicare and Medicaid. Medicare provides payment for a person who is recovering from an illness or injury. It does not provide ongoing custodial care.

Medicaid is a program jointly funded by the federal and state governments to provide assistance to the indigent who need custodial care. A third of the payments from Medicaid provide payments for the elderly who are in nursing homes. Other funds are provided for those who are disabled or without financial resources. Medicaid does not currently provide any benefits for assisted living or home care. It is strictly for those individuals who are in a nursing home.

To qualify for Medicaid, you must meet strict income and asset limitations. In 2016 the income limits range from a minimum of $2002.50 to $2980.05 depending on the state in which you live.

Monthly income limits differ depending on whether the applicant is single or married and what the community spouse's housing costs are. For a married couple, the spouse remaining in the community (community spouse) can retain all of his or her income. The community spouse's income would not be counted in determining the applicant's eligibility for Medicaid. However, all of the applicant's income must be counted for his or her long-term care except for certain deductions.

To qualify for Medicaid coverage, the recipient's countable assets cannot exceed $2000. Countable assets consist of all investments such as stocks, bonds, mutual funds, checking and savings accounts and CDs. Countable assets also include any personal or real property as well as any art and collectibles.

The amount of funds that the healthy spouse (the community spouse) is allowed to keep is called the community spouse resource allowance (CSRA), and it varies by state. Medicaid sets a minimum and maximum CSRA that the state CSRA must fall within, but the states are allowed to choose within that range. The community spouse resource allowance (CSRA) on the federal level is a minimum of $23,844 and a maximum of $119,220 in 2016. Check with your state's Medicaid agency to find out how much in resources you are allowed to keep in your state.

Based on these requirements, it is very unlikely that your client will qualify for Medicaid unless their income is very low and they have depleted all their assets in paying for care. Transferring assets to a child or trust will not qualify your clients for Medicaid if they transferred those assets within the last five years. These assets will be added back in and counted as their own.

Veteran's Long-Term Care Benefits

The Department of Veterans Affairs provides three types of long-term care benefits for veterans.

The first type is benefits provided to veterans enrolled in VA health care who have a substantial service-connected disability. These medically necessary services include home care, hospice, respite care, assisted living, domiciliary care, geriatric assessments and nursing home care.

Some of these services may be offered to veterans in the health care system who do not have service-connected disabilities but who may qualify because of low income or because they are receiving Pension income from VA. These recipients may have to provide out-of-pocket co-pays or the services may only be available to these non-service-connected disabled veterans if the regional hospital has funds to cover them.

Currently, veterans desiring to join the health care system may be refused application because their income is too high or they do not qualify under other enrollment criteria. Increased demand in recent years for services and lack of congressional funding have forced VA to allow only certain classes of veterans to join the health care system.

The second type of benefit is state veteran's homes. The U.S. Department of Veterans Affairs, in conjunction with the states, helps build and support state veteran's homes. Money is provided by VA to help share the cost of construction with the state, and a daily subsidy is provided for each veteran using nursing home care in a state home. These facilities are generally available for any veteran and sometimes the non-veteran spouse and are run by the states, often with the help of contract management. Most state veteran's homes offer nursing home care but they may also offer assisted living, domiciliary care and adult day care. There may be waiting lists for acceptance into veteran's homes in some states.

State veteran's homes are not free but are subsidized; however, the cost could be significantly less than a comparable facility in the private sector. Some of these homes can accept Medicaid payments. A complete list of state veteran's homes can be found at http://www.longtermcarelink.net/ref_state_veterans_va_nursing_homes.htm

The third type of benefit for veterans is a disability benefit. This includes benefits known as Compensation or Pension, which is also known as the Aid and Attendance benefit.

Compensation is designed to award the veteran a certain amount of monthly income to compensate for potential loss of income in the private sector due to a disability, injury or illness incurred in the service. In order to receive Compensation, a veteran has to have evidence of a service-connected disability. Most veterans who are receiving this benefit were awarded an amount based on a percentage of disability when they left the service.

However, some veterans may have a military record of being exposed to extreme cold, having an in-service non-disabling injury, having tropical diseases, tuberculosis or other incidents or exposures that at the time may not have caused any disability but years later have resulted in medical problems. In addition, some veterans may be receiving Compensation but their condition has worsened and they may qualify for a higher disability rating. Veterans mentioned above may qualify for a first-time benefit or receive an increase in Compensation amount. Applications should be submitted to see if they can receive an award. There is no income or asset test for Compensation and the benefit is non-taxable.

Pension is available to all active duty veterans who served on active duty at least 90 days, including one day beginning or ending during a period of war. There is no need to have a service-connected disability to receive Pension. To be eligible, the applicant must be totally disabled if he or she is younger than 65. Proof of disability is not required for applicants age 65 or over. Apparently, being old is evidence in itself of disability. Pension is sometimes known as the "aid and attendance benefit."

Pension can pay up to $1,789 a month for a single veteran, $1,149 per month for a surviving spouse, $2,120 a month if the veteran is married and $2,837 to two veterans who are married. This amount changes each year and is tied into the cost of living. The funds are provided to help offset the costs associated with home care, assisted living, nursing homes and other unreimbursed medical expenses. The amount of payment varies with the type of care, recipient income and the marital status of the recipient. There are income and asset tests to qualify.

Eligibility must be proven by filing the proper Veterans Application for Pension or Compensation (Form 21-534 surviving spouse, Form 21-526 Veteran).

Long-Term Care Insurance

What do you for your client if Medicare is not sufficient to cover their long-term care costs and they don't qualify for Medicaid or Veteran's benefits? Most likely they will use up their investment and retirement assets or tap into their home equity using a reverse mortgage or a home equity loan. But if you planned ahead and your clients applied for long-term care insurance while they were healthy, they would have insurance to pay for their care.

During my thirty-three years as a financial advisor, I saw many families whose retirement assets were protected because they had purchased long-term care insurance. One of my clients was working part-time as a newspaper reporter at the age of 71. Her husband was a retired executive. Based on my recommendation, they had both purchased long-term care while they were in their 60s.

Unfortunately, the husband was diagnosed with Parkinson's disease. His wife was able to care for him while he was still in the early stages of the disease. But bad luck struck their family twice. She suffered a stroke and was no longer able to take care of him or herself. Their long-term care insurance covered the cost of aides to take care of both of them at home. Every time I met with them after that they thanked me for recommending the insurance.

In the past, many advisers and financial authorities were very cynical about long-term care insurance, but that has changed dramatically in the last ten years. Long-term care insurance has improved significantly in that period of time. Companies have improved benefits and expanded coverage to provide care at home, adult daycare and assisted living facilities, as well as nursing homes.

In addition, the I.R.S. has provided additional tax incentives for individuals to own long-term care insurance. If any individual receives a long-term care benefit from an insurance company, it may be considered tax-free income. Check with your tax advisor for details. Policyholders can also deduct a portion of their premiums as a medical expense based on their age. Each year the I.R.S. publishes a table to determine the amount of your premium you can deduct.

The I.R.S. has also made it attractive for businesses to provide long-term care insurance coverage to their key people. In the traditional corporation, a business owner can select key people (including him or herself) and have the business pay for the long-term care for those employees and their spouses without it being considered taxable income to that person. In addition, the business can deduct what it spends on the premium. Finally, if any employee or spouse receives benefits from the policy, the money received is not taxable. The government has made long-term care a benefit with significant tax advantages for the employer and employee.

To qualify for payments under most long-term care policies, a doctor must certify that the person is unable to do two or more of the activities of daily living. These activities include bathing, toileting, eating, transferring in and out of bed, dressing and walking. Cognitive impairment from dementia or Alzheimer's is also covered.

The most objections to buying coverage I have heard were from those people who thought long-term care insurance was too expensive. But the cost of care is even more expensive. Here in the Northeast, the cost of a stay in an assisted living residence is between $5000-$8000 per month. Nursing homes are around $10,000 a month. These costs can deplete your investments very quickly. I think paying $3000 a year for coverage is well worth it. My wife and I bought our coverage when we were in our 50s.

If you are unwilling to paying the costs of long-term care insurance, there are other options. The industry has developed several hybrid products that provide long-term care insurance as well as other permanent benefits. One of these is a life insurance policy that incorporates long-term care insurance within it. This type of policy can be purchased with a one-time payment or in some cases an annual premium like traditional life insurance.

One of my clients told me he was not interested in paying long-term care premiums that he would never recover if he didn't need the care. He purchased a life insurance policy with a single payment of $100,000. He immediately had $165,000 of life insurance if he died. At the same time, he was able to choose a long-term care benefit equal to 2% of the death benefit for four years as part of the policy. This meant that his life insurance policy would pay up to

$3300 per month for long-term care for four years. If he did not use the long-term care benefit, the life insurance benefit would be paid out to his beneficiary at his death. If he did use the long-term care benefit, the life insurance death benefit would be reduced to a minimum guaranteed amount. In this way, he felt he was getting the full value for his premium dollars.

In addition to life insurance policies, some annuities have long-term care benefits. These annuities accumulate at a guaranteed rate of interest and build up a cash fund that can be used to pay for long-term care. As long as the interest is deferred in the annuity, you do not pay taxes on the gain. The gain is only taxed (as ordinary income) when you make withdrawals from the contract. If the cash value of the annuity is not used to pay for long-term care, you can pass on the annuity to your heirs. Unlike life insurance, however, the beneficiary must pay taxes on the gain when they receive it. Life insurance benefits are received tax-free.

Question 2. Where do you want to live if you need care?

Staying in Your Home

In a recent AARP study, nearly 75% of adults forty-five and older said they strongly desire to stay in their current home as long as possible. To make sure that your clients can "age in place," they may have to make several updates to their home and financial plan. They shouldn't wait until there is a crisis to make needed improvements.

Here are some issues to consider:
- Are their doorways wide enough to accommodate a wheelchair? A narrow wheelchair or walker needs clearance of at least 32 inches

- Do they have their master bedroom on the first floor? If not, are the steps to the second floor steep and is the stairway narrow? They may have to consider some sort of stairway elevator to get up and down at some point.
- Do they have a full bathroom on the first floor? If so does it have a walk in shower? Converting a bathtub to a walk-in shower may cost somewhere between $3000-5000. This is most likely one of their most costly changes.
- They need to review access to the home itself. In addition to the entry way being wide enough for a wheelchair or walker, is there room to install a ramp for access if necessary?

Clients shouldn't wait until someone is coming home from the hospital to consider these steps. They should look around now and start planning to make the changes that will help them stay in their home. Most of the suggestions listed above will not only make their home safe and accessible, but they will probably increase its market value as well.

Alternatives to Home Care

There are certainly other options to staying in the family home. **As 10,000 baby boomers reach retirement age every day, most who need care will not plan to enter an assisted living residence and will never step foot into a traditional nursing home.** Increasing numbers will seek out new alternatives for independent living where care can be provided.

Intentional communities for philosophical, religious, and lifestyle groups are emerging. Wikipedia describes an intentional community as "a planned residential community designed from the start to have a high degree of social cohesion and teamwork. The members of an intentional community typically hold a common social, political, religious, or spiritual vision and often follow an alternative lifestyle. They typically share responsibilities and resources."

Alex Mawhinney, a developer of retirement communities for over 25 years, reports in his article, Intentional Elder Neighborhoods, http://www.secondjourney.org/itin/2010Spr/Mawhinney_2010Spr.htm, that "intentional elder neighborhoods are becoming the new paradigm for elder living." He states that boomers will no longer be interested in "the older generation of elder living options that were available to our parents" that look like one of the following:

- Age in place - in a home not designed for aging in place, and eventually aging alone
- Move in with children or other relatives
- Move to an institution. The institution might be a nursing home, an assisted living facility, a rest home, a retirement hotel, or a continuing care retirement community with multiple levels of care.

These elder neighborhoods are taking many different forms. It would behoove you to determine if any of them have been created in your community.

There are SOTELs (service-oriented technically enhanced living, like an upscale Embassy Suites), ecovillages, senior cohousing and the new lifestyle communities like those being developed by Canyon Ranch.

The common traits of these new alternatives are that they are:
- Human-scaled (not large and impersonal)
- Relationship-based

- resident managed/centered, with an overlay of lifelong learning, later-life spirituality
- give back to the community

Question 3. Who Will Care for You?

If your client as the healthy spouse chooses to become the primary caregiver for their sick partner, it can put a very heavy burden on that spouse. As a result of caregiving for a long period of time, the healthy spouse may become a second sick spouse. Generally, caregivers provide care for their spouse for an average of four to five years. Twenty-two percent of these spousal caregivers suffer from depression.

One of my clients had a stroke at age 70. He is a very big man who was an active golfer, but he lost all the strength and movement in his right side. His wife chose to take care of him at home. She was not able to get him in and out of bed by herself, so she hired an aide to come in the morning and to come again at night. For the rest of the day she acted as his caregiver. As a result, for the last five years she has been homebound and unable to take any trips or visit any friends. She limits her time away from the home to one or two hours per day to do grocery shopping or run errands.

Many families have asked a daughter or daughter-in-law to become a caregiver to the sick parent. This puts an added burden on the family. It is even more difficult if both parents are not well and there is no family member nearby to act as the caregiver. In these cases, if you want to stay in the home, a professional aide must be hired.

The cost of a health care worker in your home is approximately $25 an hour in most areas of the country. Your clients may be able to find someone less expensive if they are very lucky, but they would have to hire them directly and not through an agency. The advantage of using an agency is that they have done some background checks on their workers and they usually have the resources to provide you with another person if the first one doesn't work out. If you hire someone directly, you take responsibility for his or her character.

It is very important for your clients to discuss with their spouse and children the difficulties of becoming a caregiver if they choose to stay in their home. Each family member must be fully aware of the challenges and responsibilities of such a role before they take it on.

FIVE

STEP FOUR: BUILDING A NETWORK OF PROFESSIONALS

It is impossible for you, as a financial advisor, to know all there is to know about the aging process and the resources available to your clients as they age. It is important to create a network of professionals to help you. These people don't need to be part of your organization but should be in your community.

Probably the first professional that you need to have access to is an elder law attorney. These are attorneys who render legal services for the benefit of the elderly, have an understanding of the aging process and are sensitive to the needs of the elderly. You can find an elder law attorney through the National Academy of Elder Law Attorneys at http://www.naela.org.

If you are not licensed to sell insurance and do not have an understanding of long-term care insurance, you should affiliate with a long-term care insurance agent. It is important to find an agent who is independent and willing to be objective in reviewing the insurance needs of a client. The Corporation for Long-term Care Certification (CLTC) has educated thousands of insurance agents to have a better understanding of long-term care insurance. You can find agents in your area through their website, http://www.ltc-cltc.com.

Another important person in your network is a Geriatric Care Manager. A professional geriatric care manager is trained to assess, plan, coordinate, monitor and provide services for the elderly and their families. They been educated in various fields of human services social work, psychology, nursing, gerontology

Geriatric Care Managers belong to the Aging Life Care Association, found online here, https://www.aginglifecare.org, and are certified by one of the three certification organizations for care management: The National Association of Social Workers, The National Academy of Certified Care Managers, or The Commission for Case Manager Certification.

These professionals can be very helpful in assessing the needs of your clients and making recommendations for services and resources.

It is also important to get to know physicians in your community who have expertise in working with the elderly. If you client is considering downsizing and selling his home, there are senior real estate specialists who concentrate on helping seniors make this transition. They will also assist in estate sales and disposing of unneeded furniture.

You will make a strong statement to your clients if you make them aware that you have a network of professionals that can help them. You will stand out from the typical financial advisor who is not conscious of the needs of older clients.

SIX

STEP FIVE: BUILDING A RELATIONSHIP WITH THE FAMILY

If your client is in the early stages of Alzheimer's or some other form of dementia, their family will need a great deal of support. It is important that you have a good relationship with the client's spouse and his adult children. At some point, you will be actively involved with them in managing your client's financial affairs.

I have found that one of the best ways to build a relationship with the family is to organize a family meeting. The family meeting can be a life changing experience for the entire family if it is conducted properly. Most families have never before gathered together as a group to discuss critical family issues. This family meeting will probably be the first time they sit down together with a specific agenda and an outside facilitator who will direct their conversation.

It is important that everyone in the family enters into this discussion with a certain level of trust and compassion. Family members are more likely to share their feelings honestly if they know they will not be verbally attacked or criticized. The purpose of the meeting is to clarify and discuss the family's plans for the future and the role each family member in dealing with the needs of mom and dad if one of them is incapacitated.

The family meeting is not the setting to bring up old conflicts between various members of the family, such as who Mom and Dad favor more, who has gotten financial help and who has not been in communication with their siblings. The focus should be on helping them discuss their options and develop a realistic course of action for the care of your failing client.

I strongly suggest that you as financial advisor be the facilitator of this meeting. You probably know more about your client's affairs than any other of their advisers. In addition, it is an excellent opportunity to get to know the adult children better and hopefully facilitate a future relationship with them.

As the facilitator, you will open up the meeting by stating some basic ground rules. These rules include the predicted length of the meeting, whether or not follow-up sessions are planned and the times of scheduled breaks. You will select a family member to act as scribe, documenting topics that were discussed, decisions that were made and follow-up that needs to happen.

It would be useful if you had conversations with each of the family members before the meeting. A phone call is usually sufficient to start to build a relationship with them and find out their concerns and opinions on what course of action should be taken. From these conversations you can build an agenda for the meeting.

Meetings shouldn't be more than a few hours long. It may be necessary to have more than one meeting. The goals of the process are to establish a course of action for the family to take and the support roles each member will take in carrying out that plan.

You will find that conducting the family meeting will dramatically reduce the anxiety within the family regarding a parent's decline. It will offer peace of mind to the healthy spouse knowing that her family will work together to support her.

Financial Advisor Safeguard, Vol. 1

I offer a free guide to Financial Advisors called, *The Financial Advisor's Guide to Organizing and Structuring Family Meetings: How to Retain the Next Generation of Your Current Clients.* **This guide is available at** http://www.FamilyMeetingChecklist.com.

SEVEN

STEP SIX: UTILIZE A SINGLE SOURCE RECORD-KEEPING DOCUMENT

As a client's memory becomes impaired, it is important for the client and his or her family to have a single source to track all important documents and information. **In fact, it is very valuable for all of your clients (and you) to establish one central location to maintain all financial records.**

During my thirty-three-year career as a financial advisor, I observed many clients who were facing a family emergency and couldn't find the important documents and information they needed to handle their affairs. If you are clients are like many of mine, their information is scattered in several different places, some of which their family doesn't even know exists. Let's get that corrected!

You have several options for collecting and maintaining your client's financial information. The method you choose is the one you are most comfortable with. Some people like the tangible quality of a traditional notebook. Others are more comfortable with an internet-based system. The most important thing is that you select a system that works for you and your clients and they regularly maintain it.

I have created a resource for my clients called The Lifefolio System® I developed it over 33 years as a financial advisor. It is in PDF format and can be transferred to a notebook, saved on a computer, in the cloud or on a flash drive. **You can obtain it at** http://www.LifeFolioSystem.com.

This primary document should include:
- Contact information for all advisors
- Where to find records and keys
- All user IDs and passwords for important Internet accounts
- Medical history and medications
- Investment and bank accounts
- Insurance products with beneficiaries
- Legal documents including wills, trusts, durable powers and health care proxies

When the document is completed, your clients will have much greater peace of mind.

EIGHT

STEP SEVEN: CREATING AN INVESTMENT POLICY STATEMENT

This statement provides the general investment goals and objectives of a client and describes the strategies that the manager should employ to meet these objectives. Specific information on matters such as asset allocation, risk tolerance, and liquidity requirements would also be included in an IPS.

The IPS is useful in reinforcing decisions jointly made by the client and advisor. The statement can be also be reviewed by the client's advocate and family members to make certain that it is appropriate. It also protects the advisor, in case anyone questions his intentions.

An IPS usually has five major components that should be unique to each client.

1. All key factual data about the client, including where the client's assets are held, the amount of their assets under your management, and the identification of the trustees or interested parties to the account. This can be as detailed or as simple as desired.

2. A discussion and review of the client's investment objectives, investment time horizon, anticipated withdrawals or deposits, need for reserves or liquidity, and attitudes regarding tolerance for risk and volatility.

3. Any constraints and restrictions on the assets, such as liquidity and marketability requirements, diversification concentrations, the advisor's investment strategy (including tax management), locations of assets by account type (taxable versus tax-deferred), how client accounts that are not being managed (if any) will be handled, and any transaction prohibitions.

4. The security types and asset classes to be included in or excluded from the portfolio, and the basic allocation among asset categories and the variance (rebalancing) limits for this allocation.

5. The monitoring and control procedures and responsibilities of each party.

The Investment Policy Statement is a guide for the advisor and the client, keeping them focused on the objectives of the client's investment program.

NINE

CONCLUDING THOUGHTS

If you follow these seven steps that I have outlined, you will protect yourself and your client if he or she ever loses his or her mental capacity. Take the time to complete them and you will be far ahead of your peers.

Your efforts will also distinguish you as the trusted advisor for the entire family. You will be among the few advisors who go beyond the traditional limits of financial planning and create lasting relationships with future generations. Research has shown that 94% of accounts currently go to a new advisor when a client dies. The adult children don't normally have a relationship with their parents' advisor.

I am confident that if you provide the services that I have suggested in this book you will reduce this statistic dramatically. You will create a relationship with the adult children, making it much more likely for them to work with you.

Don't forget to grab my free gift to you, *The LifeFolio System®: Six Steps to Organizing Your Life with the LifeFolio System®*. It will help you get all of your important papers and information in order before disaster strikes. **It is available for download at http://www.LifeFolioSystem.com.**

About Bob Mauterstock

Bob Mauterstock is an accomplished speaker, author and sought after authority on the financial concerns of baby boomers and their adult children. Bob is the author of two books, *Can We Talk? The Financial Guide for Baby Boomers Assisting Their Elderly Parents* and *Passing the Torch, Critical Conversations with Your Adult Children*.

For over 35 years, Bob has helped families achieve a worry-free, comfortable retirement. He has inspired baby boomers and their adult children to give each other the gift of communication and preserve their legacy for future generations.

Bob holds a Master's Degree in Education from University of Connecticut and a Bachelor's Degree in Psychology from Princeton University. He is a former Navy helicopter pilot and holds the CFP®, ChFC, and CLTC designations.

He has been quoted in a number of publications and appeared on several radio programs. In addition, he has spoken to groups of financial advisors and their clients throughout the country.

Bob is an active member of the Financial Planning Association. He serves on the Board of Directors for Cape Mediation, and the

Brewster Ladies' Library, He is a member of the Academy of Model Aeronautics and the Nauset Newcomers.

In his play time, he flies model airplanes and creates aerial videos with his quadcopter.

Bob has prepared and presented a number of programs for financial advisors and their clients. They include:

Working with Clients with Diminished Capacity

What do you do when you discover that one of your clients has a diminished mental capacity? According to the Alzheimer's Association, Alzheimer's disease will strike more than 8 million Americans by 2030 (a rise of 60% from 2010). If you don't know what steps to take to protect your client and your practice, both may be at risk. Bob has developed a protocol that you can follow to deal with this problem. Attend his workshop and learn the steps you can take to help your aging clients and preserve the business you have worked so hard to build.

Passing the Torch, Critical Conversations Your Clients Must Have

Boomers are concerned about the conversations they need to have with their adult children about all the issues they will face as they get older. Passing the Torch gives you, as their advisor, a practical and empathetic approach to help them work with their children to discuss and plan all the decisions they will have to make. This workshop lays out the steps to prepare and hold a family meeting to open up the lines of communication. It addresses such critical areas as legal issues that can impact the family, end of life planning, health care planning and passing on a legacy to the next generation.

Financial Advisor Safeguard, Vol. 1

Workshop for Your Clients: Critical Conversations You Must Have with Your Family

Bob has presented a number of workshops to advisors' clients to give the advisor additional credibility and add value to their relationship. In these workshops he includes the following topics:

- simple techniques to bridge the communication gap between generations
- understanding the critical issues that are most important to the family
- the 5 essential legal issues that boomers must address
- how to create a long-term care plan for the family
- 7 tips for gathering and organizing the critical information clients need to plan for the future.

Contact Bob if you are interested in him making a presentation to your advisors or your clients. Email him at: bob@giftofcommunication.com

WEBSITE: http://www.GiftofCommunication.com
FACEBOOK: https://www.facebook.com/giftofcommunication
TWITTER: https://twitter.com/rmauterstock
LINKEDIN: https://www.linkedin.com/in/rmauterstock

www.ingramcontent.com/pod-product-compliance
Lightning Source LLC
Chambersburg PA
CBHW070416190526
45169CB00003B/1280